HOUGHTON MIFFLIN

Discover

INVITATIONS
TO LITERACY

Houghton Mifflin Company • Boston

Atlanta • Dallas • Geneva, Illinois • Palo Alto • Princeton

Reading Is An Adventure
That Makes Every Day Special

Book Adventure™
www.bookadventure.org

read.
Use the on-line "Book Finder" to find a book you want to read.

click.
After reading, return on-line to take a fun interactive quiz.

win.
For every correct answer, you can earn points. Redeem the points for prizes.

When you read, use these Reading Strategies to become a better reader.

- Predict/Infer
- Think About Words
- Self-Question

- Monitor
- Evaluate
- Summarize

HOUGHTON MIFFLIN

Discover

Senior Authors

J. David Cooper
John J. Pikulski

Authors

Kathryn H. Au
Margarita Calderón
Jacqueline C. Comas
Marjorie Y. Lipson
J. Sabrina Mims
Susan E. Page
Sheila W. Valencia
MaryEllen Vogt

Consultants

Dolores Malcolm
Tina Saldivar
Shane Templeton

INVITATIONS TO LITERACY

Houghton Mifflin Company • Boston

Atlanta • Dallas • Geneva, Illinois • Palo Alto • Princeton

Cover and title page photography by Tim Turner.

Cover illustration from *Fish Faces* by Norbert Wu. Copyright © 1993 by Norbert Wu. Reprinted by permission of Henry Holt & Company.

Acknowledgments appear on page 223.

Printed in the U.S.A.

ISBN: 0-618-05783-8

23456789-VH-05 04 03 02 01 00

CONTENTS

Family Treasures

BIG BOOK **PLUS**

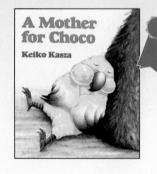
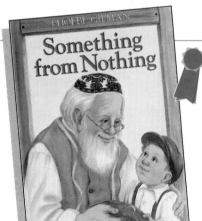

CONTENTS

Something

Fishy

BIG BOOK **PLUS**

Fishy Facts
nonfiction written and illustrated by
Ivan Chermayeff
In the same book . . .
a science activity, fish poems, and fine art

Anthology

PAPERBACK **PLUS**

Meet the Author
Marilee Robin Burton

♦ ♦ ♦ ♦ ♦

Marilee Robin Burton loves shoes! When she was a teacher, Ms. Burton would do a shoe project every year with her class. Her students would tell her stories about their favorite shoes.

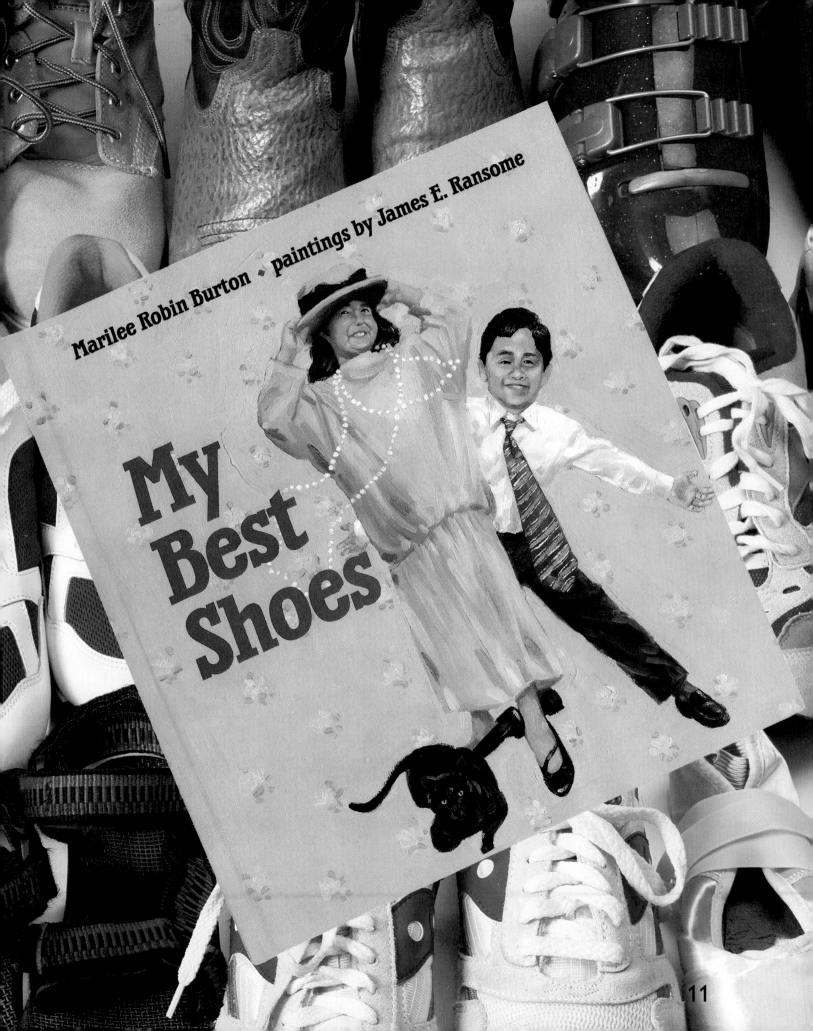

Marilee Robin Burton • paintings by James E. Ransome

My
Best
Shoes

On Monday I wore tie shoes
Sturdy lace up high shoes
Tie them in a bow shoes
Knot them in a tangle shoes

13

Oops . . . don't let them dangle shoes.

On Tuesday I wore tap shoes

Buckle and strap shoes
With one little snap shoes
Learn how to dance shoes
Twirl and prance shoes.

On Wednesday I wore play shoes

Gray shoes

Run all day shoes

Race, skip, and hop shoes

Jump and then stop shoes.

On Thursday I wore old shoes

Dirty brown and gold shoes

Scratched and scuffed and muffed shoes

Scruffed shoes

Not polished or buffed shoes.

On Friday I wore new shoes
Bright and shiny blue shoes
Twinkling in the light shoes
Sparkling in the night shoes

What a pretty sight shoes!

On Saturday I wore sun shoes

Just for fun shoes

Tiptoe in the sand shoes

Water, grass, and land shoes

Carry in my hand shoes.

On Sunday I wore no shoes

Naked feet and toe shoes

Barefoot all day long shoes

Sing a summer song shoes

Can't go wrong shoes. . . .

They're my very best!

Meet the Illustrator
James E. Ransome

◆ ◆ ◆ ◆ ◆

James E. Ransome also loves shoes! Here is a painting of his favorite shoes, a pair of green sneakers. These sneakers are on the back cover of *My Best Shoes*.

Mr. Ransome lives in New York with his wife, Lesa, his daughter, Jaime, and his Dalmatian, Clinton.

Your Best Shoes

What kind of shoes would you like to wear? Make your own special shoes!

jumping shoe

climbing shoe

Family Treasures

A Mother for Choco

Keiko Kasza

A Mother for Choco
by Keiko Kasza

Table of Contents

More Books You Can Read!

PHONICS BOOKSHELF

First Time in the Sky

PHONICS BOOKSHELF

The New Soup

PHONICS BOOKSHELF

My Older Sister

WATCH **ME** READ

Looking After Billy

WATCH **ME** READ

Ned's New Old Sled

WATCH **ME** READ

A Moon for Ana Gracia

ON MOTHER'S LAP
By Ann Herbert Scott
illustrated by Glo Coalson

PAPERBACK **PLUS**

Meet
Phoebe Gilman

Here are two photos of Phoebe Gilman. The photo on the left shows her with her brothers and cousins when she was a little girl.

Today, she loves to visit classrooms. In the photo on the right, she is reading a book to a group of students.

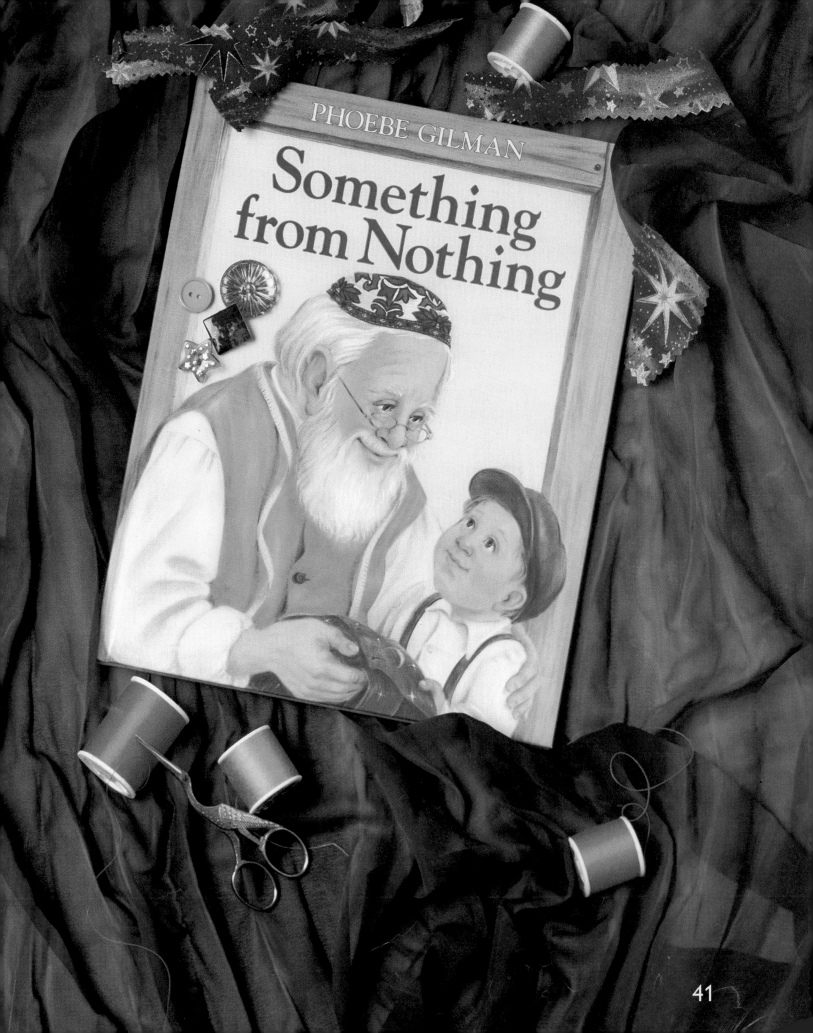

For Irving Hirschhorn
Our Uncle
We remember you with love.

When Joseph was a baby, his grandfather
made him a wonderful blanket . . .

. . . to keep him warm and cozy and to chase away bad dreams.

But as Joseph grew older, the wonderful blanket grew older too.

One day his mother said to him, "Joseph, look at your blanket. It's frazzled, it's worn, it's unsightly, it's torn. It is time to throw it out."

"Grandpa can fix it," Joseph said.

Joseph's grandfather took the blanket and turned
it round and round.

"Hmm," he said as his scissors went snip, snip, snip and his needle flew in and out and in and out, "There's just enough material here to make . . ." ⟨47⟩

. . . a wonderful jacket. Joseph put on the wonderful jacket and went outside to play.

But as Joseph grew older, the wonderful jacket grew older too.

48

One day his mother said to him, "Joseph, look at your jacket. It's shrunken and small, doesn't fit you at all. It is time to throw it out!"

"Grandpa can fix it," Joseph said.
Joseph's grandfather took the jacket and turned
it round and round.

"Hmm," he said as his scissors went snip, snip, snip and his needle flew in and out and in and out, "There's just enough material here to make . . ." ⟨51⟩

. . . a wonderful vest. Joseph wore the wonderful vest to school the very next day.

But as Joseph grew older, the wonderful vest grew older too.

One day his mother said to him, "Joseph, look at
your vest! It's spotted with glue and there's paint
on it too. It is time to throw it out!"

"Grandpa can fix it," Joseph said.
Joseph's grandfather took the vest and turned it
round and round.

"Hmm," he said as his scissors went snip, snip, snip and his needle flew in and out and in and out, "There's just enough material here to make . . ."

55

. . . a wonderful tie. Joseph wore the wonderful tie to his grandparents' house every Friday.

But as Joseph grew older, his wonderful tie grew older too.

One day his mother said to him, "Joseph, look at your tie! This big stain of soup makes the end of it droop. It is time to throw it out!"

"Grandpa can fix it," Joseph said.

Joseph's grandfather took the tie and turned it round and round.

"Hmm," he said as his scissors went snip, snip, snip and his needle flew in and out and in and out, "There's just enough material here to make . . ." 59

. . . a wonderful handkerchief. Joseph used the wonderful handkerchief to keep his pebble collection safe.

But as Joseph grew older, his wonderful handkerchief grew older too.

One day his mother said to him, "Joseph, look
at your handkerchief! It's been used till it's
tattered, it's splotched and it's splattered. It is time
to THROW IT OUT!"

"Grandpa can fix it," Joseph said.
Joseph's grandfather took the handkerchief and
turned it round and round.

"Hmm," he said as his scissors went snip, snip, snip and his needle flew in and out and in and out, "There's just enough material here to make . . ." ◇63◇

. . . a wonderful button. Joseph wore the wonderful button on his suspenders to hold his pants up.

One day his mother said to him, "Joseph, where
is your button?"

Joseph looked. It was gone!

He searched everywhere but he could not find it.
Joseph ran down to his grandfather's house.

"My button! My wonderful button is lost!"
His mother ran after him. "Joseph! Listen to me.

"The button is gone, finished, kaput. Even your grandfather can't make something from nothing."

Joseph's grandfather shook his head sadly. "I'm afraid that your mother is right," he said.

The next day Joseph went to school. "Hmm," he said, as his pen went scritch scratch, scritch scratch, over the paper. "There's just enough material here to make . . ."

. . . a wonderful story.

Picture This!

Draw a picture of each thing Joseph's grandfather made for him.

Label each picture.

3

Then tell the story again, using your drawings.

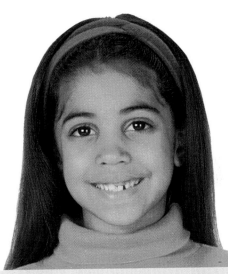

Abuelita

Quién subiera tan alto
como la luna
para ver las estrellas
una por una,
y elegir entre todas
la más bonita
para alumbrar el cuarto
de la abuelita.

por Tomás Allende Iragorri

Grandma

I wish I could fly as high
as the moon
to see the stars
one by one,
and pick the prettiest
one of all
to light up
Grandma's room.

by Tomás Allende Iragorri
translated from the Spanish

What's It Like to Have

Hi! We're the Christie family. We've traveled from all over the United States, from Alaska to Florida, to join our family reunion.

We meet new friends.

We swim together.

We play games together.

a Family Reunion?

We play sports together.

We eat together.

We say goodbye.

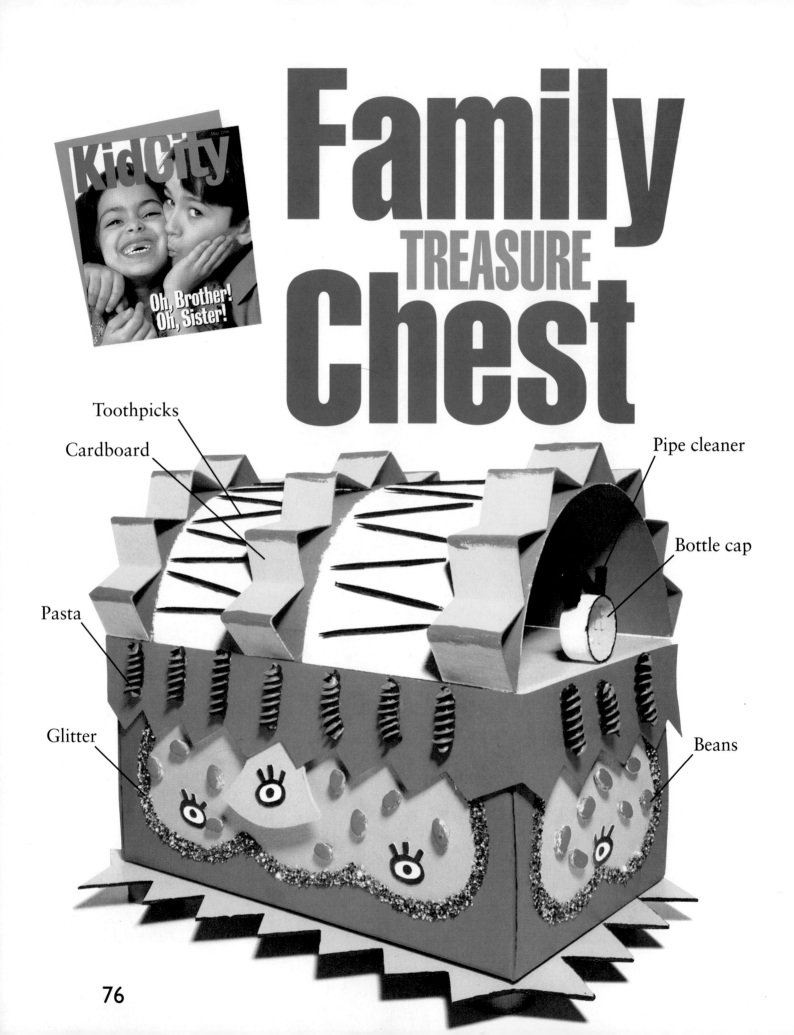

KidCity

May 1994

Oh, Brother!
Oh, Sister!

Family
TREASURE
Chest

Toothpicks

Cardboard

Pipe cleaner

Bottle cap

Pasta

Glitter

Beans

Make Your Own Treasure Chest

Need a place to save all of your special things? How about making your own family treasure chest? Remember, any special thing you have can be a family treasure!

1 Cover a shoebox with pieces of colored paper.

2 Paste things like pasta, beans, or glitter on your treasure chest.

Meet the Author
Angela Johnson

Angela Johnson comes from a family of storytellers. "I am amazed that my father and grandfather could tell my brothers and me a story a thousand times," she says. After a while, she and her brothers would know the stories by heart.

Meet the Illustrator
David Soman

David Soman has always loved to draw and paint. When he was a little boy, he spent most of his time drawing his own monsters and superheroes.

Mr. Soman lives in New York City. The city streets helped him with the drawings for *One of Three*.

ANGELA JOHNSON
One of Three
pictures by
DAVID SOMAN

Since I can remember I've been one of three.
Eva, Nikki, and me.

One of three sisters that walk to school together.
Down the street together.
One of the three in the sun and the rain.

I'm one of the three that lives in apartment number 2,
has long hair and brown eyes, and can sometimes
play hopscotch by the trash cans
if I ask for a long time.

On Saturdays I'm one of the three that sits
outside the bakery and looks and smells and smells. . . .

I'm one of the three that squeezes into the taxi
on snowy days with Mama, Aunt Sara, and Grandma,
and it's warm there.

I'm one of the three that looks just like our mama,
smiles just like our daddy,
and holds hands with my sisters in the store,
looking like triplets — almost.

I'm one of the three that likes the subway,
the people on it,
and the way our feet hang over the seats.

I'm one of three who lives over the flower shop.
Mr. Lowen still gets all of our names wrong,
but he gives us each a daisy every time.

We walk down the street like stairsteps,
and I'm in front.

97

Sometimes Eva and Nikki say I'm not
invited to go with them.
Not to the park, the store, or sometimes
even for a walk.

I'm left behind.
Not one of three, just one.

Then Mama calls me Sister and says I'm too little
to go there or do that,
so maybe I just want to help her paint or read to her.

Daddy says that I have to be the baby sometimes,
and keep Mama and him company,
just sometimes.

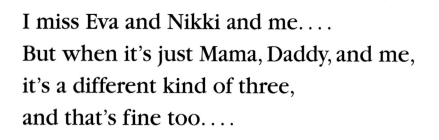

I miss Eva and Nikki and me. . . .
But when it's just Mama, Daddy, and me,
it's a different kind of three,
and that's fine too. . . .

Draw a Map

Think of all the places the girl talked about and visited in the story. What do you think her neighborhood looked like? Draw a map.

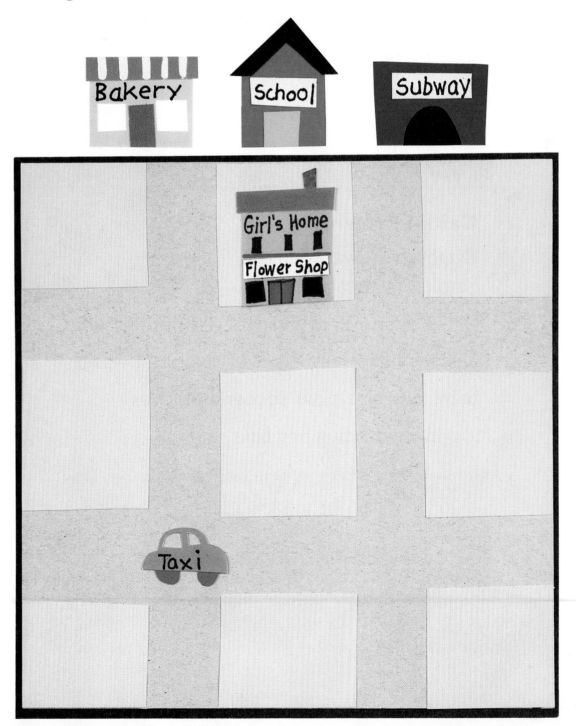

109

A NORTHWEST TRIP

A Story About Me
by Caitlin Brownrigg

Caitlin loves the outdoors and camping. What a great idea for a story about her and her family!

Caitlin Brownrigg

Elizabeth Stewart School
Pinole, California

Caitlin wrote this story about herself. She has been camping ever since she was a baby. She also plays soccer and loves jogging and riding her bike.

A Northwest Trip

My family and I went up to Washington in our pickup. We camped out. In the morning we went to the lake. We swam in the cold water. I met a girl named Hannah. We played on the beach.

Hannh

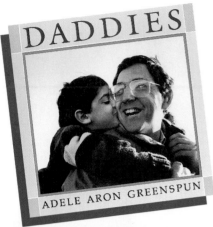

Daddies

by Adele Aron Greenspun

Daddies hold babies,
push strollers,
share feelings,
read stories.

Daddies give hugs
and kisses,
tickles and giggles,
piggyback rides.

catch and throw,

win and lose.

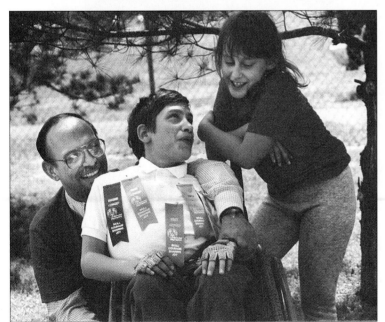

Daddies need hugs and kisses, smiles
and tickles, jokes and giggles, and . . .

"I love you."

FAMILY CIRCUS

by Bil Keane

"Has anyone seen the floor?"

Family Portraits

Many artists like to paint pictures of families. Here are some family portraits and the titles the artists gave them. What would you include in your own family portrait?

Title: **Eskimo Family**
by *John Kailukiak*

Title: **Family Portrait**
by María Izquierdo

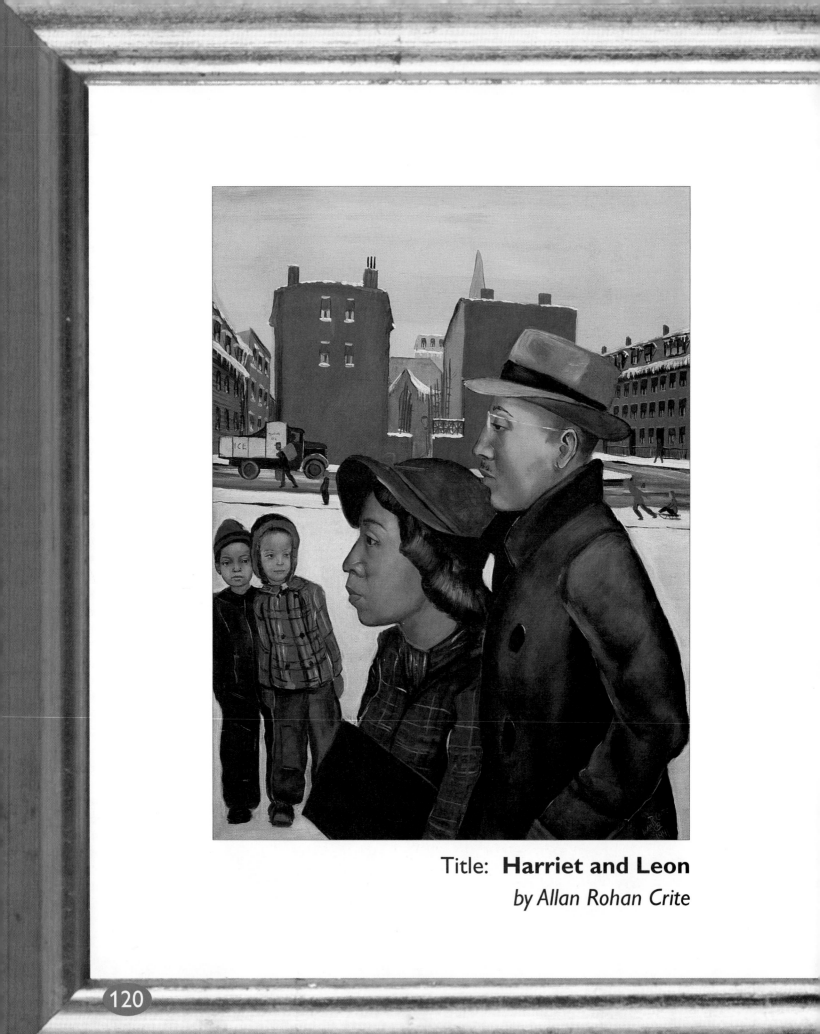

Title: **Harriet and Leon**
by Allan Rohan Crite

Title: **Home for Thanksgiving**

by Norman Rockwell

Now draw your own family portrait. Make sure you give your portrait a title.

Something

Fishy

122

Fishy Facts

Ivan Chermayeff

BIG BOOK **PLUS**

Fishy Facts

by Ivan Chermayeff

Table of Contents

More Books You Can Read!

PHONICS BOOKSHELF
Too Many Dishes for Peaches

PHONICS BOOKSHELF
Littlest Friend, Greatest Friend

PHONICS BOOKSHELF
Shark at the Shore

Is This a House for **Hermit Crab?**
by Megan McDonald
illustrated by S. D. Schindler

WATCH ME READ
Fishing with Grandpa

WATCH ME READ
Three Wishes for Buster

WATCH ME READ
What Seahorse Saw

PAPERBACK **PLUS**

ENZO the WONDERFISH

By Cathy Wilcox

I had always wanted a pet.
A pet, not quite as smart as me,
that I could feed and care for and pat.

I was the littlest.

It was always me
who was poked and prodded,
tickled and teased,
but sometimes I was cuddled.

Mom and Dad said,
"No more brothers and sisters."

That was fine with me —
if we could just get a pet.

First, I asked for a horse.

But Dad said, "Where would we keep it?"

Then, I begged for a dog.

"It's not fair to have a dog
when no one is home all day," said Mom.

"What about a cat?"

Dad scratched his whiskers.
"I think your sister's allergic," he said,
then sneaked away
without even telling me
what a *lergic* meant.

"A bird? They're cheap."

"No, I can't stand to see
a bird in a cage," said Mom,
and flew off in a huff.

"How about a rat?"
my brother asked, snickering.

But I thought one rat
in the family was enough.

I kept on trying,
but there were all sorts of reasons
why goats
and ducks
and guinea pigs
and mice
couldn't be my pets.

Then, on my seventh birthday,
my family shouted, "SURPRISE!"
and handed me my present in a bowl.

That was Enzo.
Cold and wet and goggle-eyed
and . . . my pet.

"There," said Dad,
"a fish is just as good as any other pet."

"You wait!" I told them all.

"I'll teach him to perform great feats!"

He'll be Enzo the Great!

Enzo the Magnificent! Enzo . . . the Wonderfish!"

I didn't want Enzo to feel lonely,
so I put him on my shelf
next to my family of wooden dolls.

I put my lamp above him —
a wonderfish has to get used
to being in the spotlight.

I went to the library and took out a book for me and Enzo called *Training Your Pet*.

I looked for the section on
Tricks for Fish, but there wasn't one.
Somebody must have torn it out.

"Never mind," I told Enzo.

There were plenty of things to learn,
like *fetch* and *heel* and *stay*.

I found a very tiny stick
to throw for Enzo.

"Fetch, Enzo!"

The stick floated but
Enzo just swam around it.

"Get the ball, Enzo!"

Enzo showed no interest at all
in retrieving it.

I decided to try
something easier,
so I took Enzo for a walk.

The water slopped and splashed
along the sidewalk.

I don't know if fish get seasick,
but Enzo looked as though he was.
I took him home.

There were still so many tricks
for Enzo to learn,
but there was no point in moving too fast.
I'd take it step by step.

Maybe if I showed him how,
he could master
some simple commands.

"Sit," I said, sitting down
as fishily as I could.
Enzo kept swimming.

"Beg," I said,
showing him
how to hold
his fins.

Enzo kept swimming.

"Roll over!" "Down!" "Come!" "Stay!" "Play dead!"

I showed him
all the tricks
but it was no use.

144

Enzo just wasn't interested.
All he wanted to do was swim
and blow bubbles
like some *ordinary* fish.

I needed a rest from training Enzo.
Maybe Enzo needed a rest, too.

I raced outside without even saying, "Stay!"

After dinner I went back
to my room and my shelf and the bowl
and my pet fish, Enzo.

I looked behind the books,
but Enzo wasn't there.

I looked inside the wooden dolls one by one,
but he wasn't there either.

I looked along the shelf,
and on my desk,
and on the floor,
but he wasn't anywhere.

The library book was open
to the page on leaping.

Enzo must have leapt.
But where?

150

He wasn't in my paintbrush holder
or in my ink bottle
or in my mug of crayons.

Then I found him,
floating in my teacup,
not moving at all.

"Mom! Dad! Everybody!
I think Enzo's dead."

Everyone came to look.

Dad fished Enzo out of the teacup,
and dropped him, *plop,* back in his bowl,
where he floated sideways.

"It's my fault," I said.
"I shouldn't have pushed him so hard."

"No, dear," said Mom, "don't blame yourself.
Fish sometimes jump."

And she cuddled me.

Just then, something moved in Enzo's bowl.
It was Enzo!

He was right-side up and swimming again!

Enzo flashed me a knowing look
that told me he'd just learned his second trick:

Playing dead!

Meet Cathy Wilcox

Cathy Wilcox says that she wrote *Enzo the Wonderfish* because she wanted to write a book about a pet. She used to have a pet mouse when she was a little girl, even though she had always wanted a bigger pet.

157

Funny Fish Tricks

Think of other tricks the girl could teach Enzo. Make a "Funny Fish Tricks" class book.

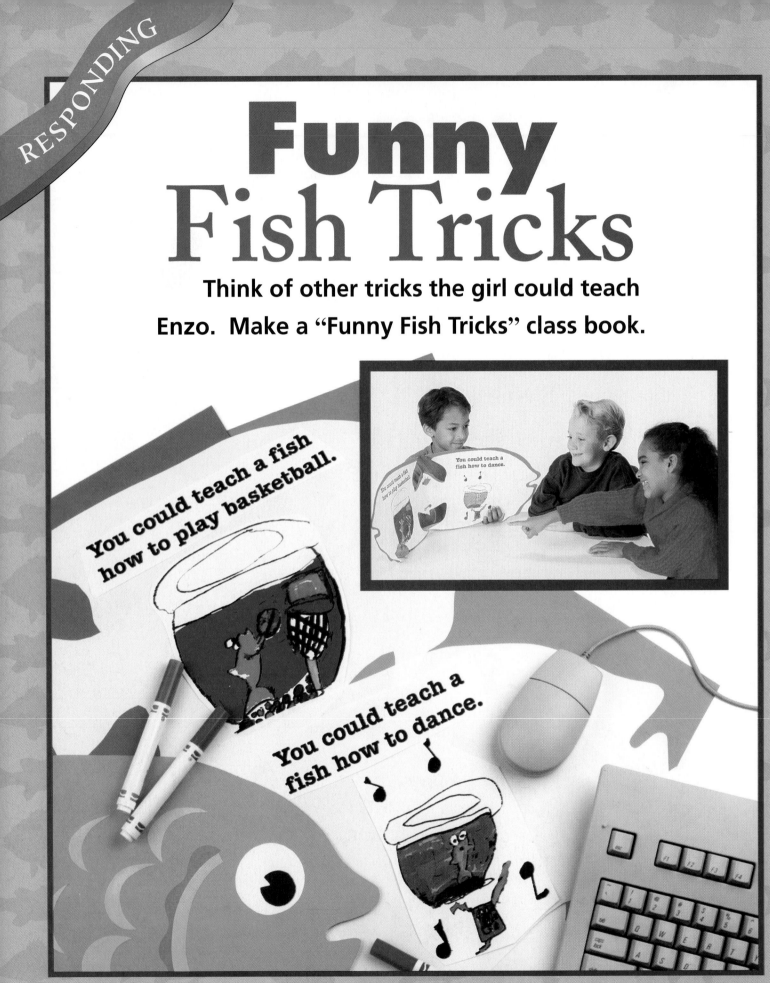

You could teach a fish how to play basketball.

You could teach a fish how to dance.

Wish

If I could wish,

I'd be a fish

(For just a day or two)

To flip and flash

And dart and splash

And nothing else to do,

And never anyone to say,

"Are you quite sure you

washed today?"

I'd like it, wouldn't you?

by Dorothy Brown Thompson

159

SHARKS

by Erik D. Stoops and Sherrie Stoops

The best-known shark of all is the great white. It is one of the largest hunters. ▶

cookie cutter shark

Sharks, just like people, come in all shapes and sizes. They live in different waters all over the world.

goblin shark

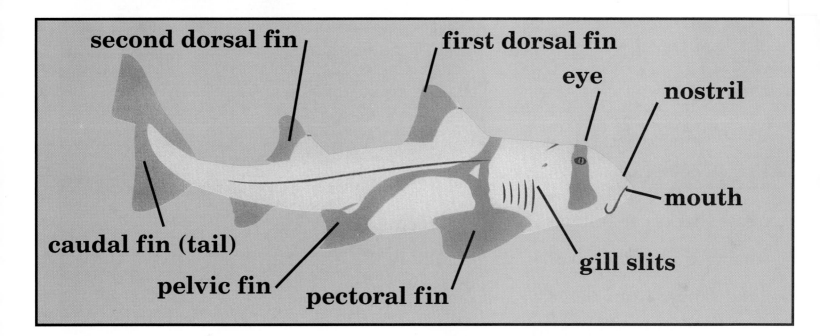

second dorsal fin

first dorsal fin

eye

nostril

mouth

gill slits

pectoral fin

pelvic fin

caudal fin (tail)

wobbegong shark

zebra shark

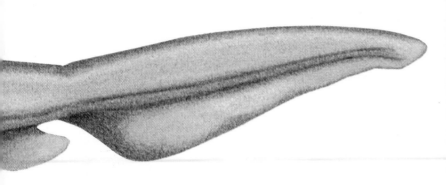

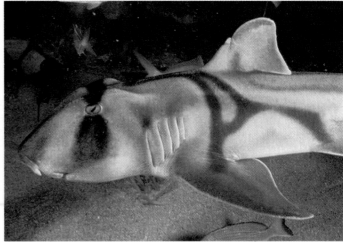

Port Jackson shark

What do sharks usually eat?

Most sharks eat animals smaller than themselves. That ranges from clams, shrimp, squid, and fish to sea turtles and seabirds. Some sharks eat large mammals, such as sea lions, dolphins, and even dead or dying whales. Some eat only plankton (tiny drifting animals and plants).

▲ **This blue shark eats mackerel, a type of fish.**

The whale shark may have a huge mouth, but it eats only small fish. ▶

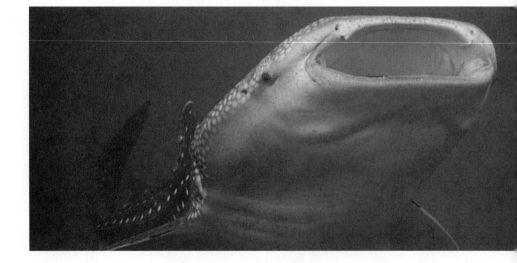

Do sharks ever lose their teeth?

Yes, they lose many thousands of teeth in a lifetime. Their teeth either fall out or are pushed out. They also lose teeth while feeding. But about every two weeks sharks get a new set of teeth.

mako shark teeth

This shark from long ago had jaws big enough to stand in. ▼

inside a tiger shark's jaw

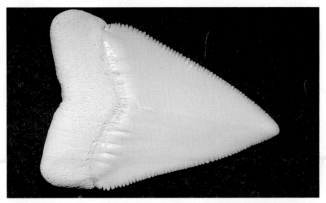

great white shark tooth

SHARKS

A Report by Cortlan Carrillo

There's so much to learn about sharks. Read what Cortlan found out about them!

Cortlan Carrillo

Perry Elementary School
Perry, Georgia

Cortlan wrote this report because he wanted to learn more about sharks. He loves to read. Cortlan's favorite stories are the Arthur books by Marc Brown. Cortlan also likes to do the math calendar at school.

ERIK D. STOOPS &
SHERRIE STOOPS

Sharks

Sharks have many rows of teeth. Some sharks have flat teeth, and some have sharp teeth. Some sharks eat turtles, and others eat dolphins. Not all sharks are mean, but great white sharks sometimes attack swimmers.

Fishy Tongue Twisters

by Alvin Schwartz

Six sharp smart sharks!

She sells seashells
by the seashore.

1/2 OFF

Five fat frogs fled
from fifty fierce fish.

167

Meet Leo Lionni

One day on a long train ride, Leo Lionni began to tell a story to his grandchildren. He made drawings to help tell it. The story later became his first picture book. The book was called *Little Blue and Little Yellow*. Since then, Mr. Lionni has written other books for children, including *Swimmy*.

A happy school of little fish lived in a corner of the sea somewhere. They were all red. Only one of them was as black as a mussel shell. He swam faster than his brothers and sisters. His name was Swimmy.

One bad day a tuna fish, swift, fierce and very hungry, came darting through the waves. In one gulp he swallowed all the little red fish. Only Swimmy escaped.

He swam away in the deep wet world. He was scared, lonely, and very sad.

But the sea was full of wonderful creatures, and as he swam from marvel to marvel Swimmy was happy again.

He saw a medusa made of rainbow jelly...

a lobster, who walked about like a water-moving machine . . .

strange fish, pulled by an invisible thread . . .

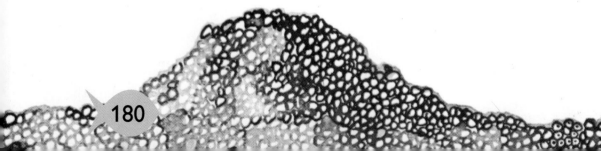

a forest of seaweeds growing from sugar-candy rocks . . .

an eel whose tail was almost too far away to remember...

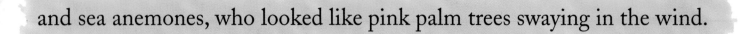

and sea anemones, who looked like pink palm trees swaying in the wind.

Then, hidden in the dark shade of rocks and weeds, he saw a school of little fish, just like his own.

"Let's go and swim and play and SEE things!" he said happily. "We can't," said the little red fish. "The big fish will eat us all."

"But you can't just lie there," said Swimmy. "We must THINK of something."

189

Swimmy thought and thought and thought.

Then suddenly he said, "I have it!"
"We are going to swim all together like the biggest fish in the sea!"

He taught them to swim close together, each in his own place,

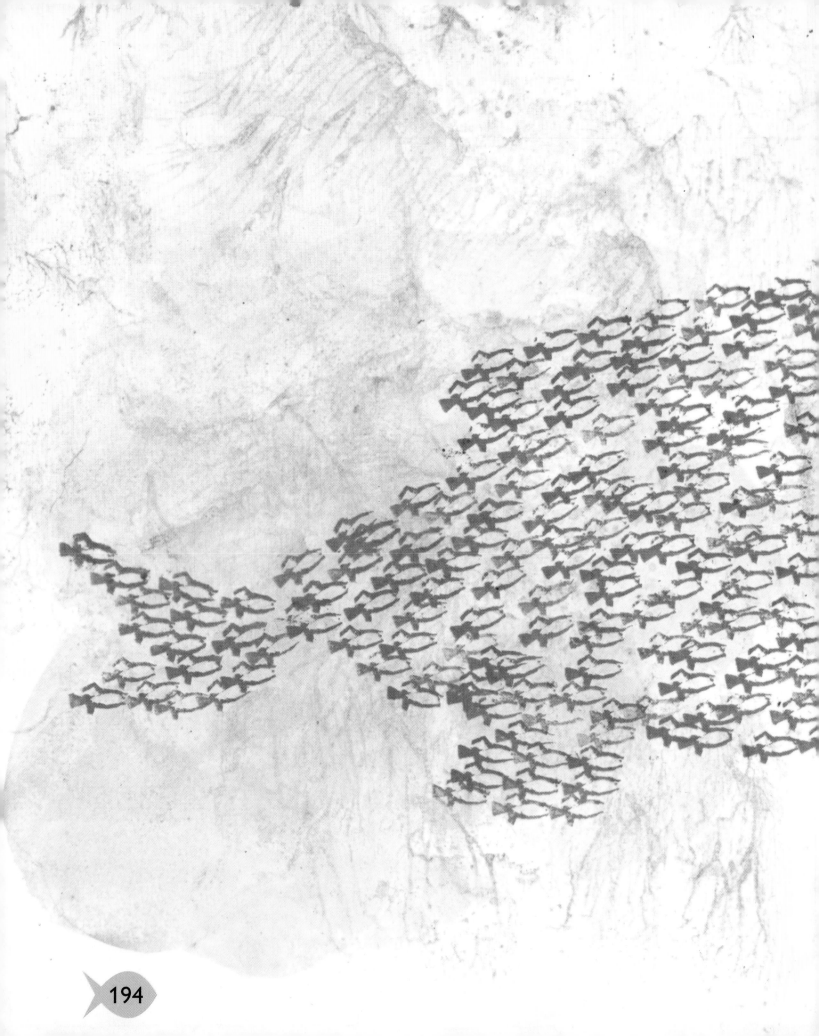

and when they had learned to swim like one giant fish, he said, "I'll be the eye."

And so they swam in the cool morning water and in the midday sun and

chased the big fish away.

HOORAY
for Swimmy!

Make an award for Swimmy. Be sure to tell why he deserves to win your award.

Best Thinker Award To Swimmy For Solving a Big Problem.

Swimmy is #1.

A brave fish

He saved his friends!

198

A la víbora de la mar

A la víbora, víbora de la mar,
por aquí van a pasar;
los de adelante corren mucho,
los de atrás se quedarán.

The Snake in the Sea

Like the snake, snake in the sea,
Through this bridge pass rapidly;
Those in front will run through fast,
Those in back will run through last.

What's it like to work at an aquarium?
Ask Rhona St. Clair

Rhona St. Clair trained seals at the New Jersey State Aquarium. She is now back at school, learning more about marine life.

Why did you become an aquarium worker?

When I was young, I watched nature shows with my father. I always wanted to learn more about animals.

Why did you work with seals?

There are no bars to keep you away from them. You can get close to them.

What was your day like?

It was very busy! I was in charge of the trainers. I also made sure that the seals' food was clean and that they ate the right amount of food.

Rhona St. Clair with seals Kara (left) and Kjya (right)

Kjya, a female gray seal

Kjya, grabbing a
Frisbee

Rhona St. Clair,
checking Squeegee's
teeth

FISH FACES

by Norbert Wu

One fish, two fish,

three fish, more

Spotted fish, dotted fish

Fish with lines and stripes and waves

One fish, two fish, three fish, four
Deep in the ocean, there are thousands more!

SEA SCHOOL

by W. Lynn Seldon, Jr.

Naomi Ruza grew up on Bonaire, a small island in the Caribbean Sea near Venezuela, South America. Naomi learned to snorkel when she was five. When she turned ten, she taught snorkeling to kids who visited the island.

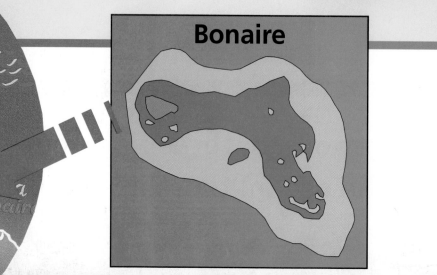

Bonaire

Naomi shows kids how to fit their masks against their faces, so no water leaks inside. Now it's time to go snorkeling!

Snorkeling gets its name from the plastic breathing tube, called a snorkel. Swimmers can float face down in the water and breathe fresh air from the tube. They look at underwater life through a face mask. Fins on their feet make them faster, stronger swimmers.

209

Once everyone is set with fins, mask, and snorkel, Naomi takes them on a tour of the world underwater. Naomi and her snorkeling students look for colorful fish and coral reefs.

Snorkelers who want a close-up look at something on the bottom take a deep breath, head down, and kick to the bottom. They hold their breath underwater. When they rise to the top, they blow a big puff of air through the snorkel to clear it.

GLOSSARY

A

allergic   When you are **allergic** to something, you may sneeze or get a rash: Ana is **allergic** to cats. She sneezes whenever she is near a cat.

apartment   An **apartment** is a home that is part of a building: My friend lives in an **apartment** on the second floor.

C

command   A **command** tells someone to do something right away: I give my dog **commands** such as "Sit!" "Roll over!" and "Stay!"

company   When you keep someone **company**, you stay with the person: When Dad takes the car to the car wash, I keep him **company** so he does not have to wait by himself.

creature   A **creature** is another name for an animal: Little fish and big whales are some of the **creatures** that live in the sea.

cuddle   When you **cuddle** someone or something, you hold it in your arms: The father **cuddled** the baby.

daddy   **Daddy** is another way to say Father or Dad: On Saturdays, I help my **daddy** do work in the yard. He likes it when I help him.

daisy   A **daisy** is a small white flower with a yellow center: I picked a **daisy** from the garden for my grandma.

feat   The people climbed the mountain. It was a great **feat** because no one thought that they could do it.

fetch   To run quickly to get something is to **fetch** it: The dog likes to **fetch** the ball.

float   When something can **float**, it can stay on top
              of the water and not sink: The toy boat
              floated on the lake. It did not sink.

handkerchief   A **handkerchief** is a small
                   cloth: I keep my
                   handkerchief in my pocket.

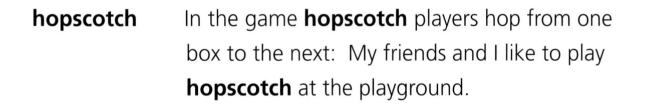

hopscotch   In the game **hopscotch** players hop from one
                box to the next: My friends and I like to play
                hopscotch at the playground.

invisible   When something is **invisible**, you cannot
                see it: Air is **invisible**.

knot   When you **knot** strings, you tie the strings together so they won't come loose: I **knot** my shoestrings so they won't open up while I walk.

M

Mama   **Mama** is another name for Mother or Mom: David calls his mother **Mama**.

marvel   A **marvel** is a wonderful thing: At the theme park, we saw a **marvel**. It was a castle made of ice.

material   **1. Material** is what something is made of: Cloth is the **material** used to make a shirt. Wood is the **material** used to make a table. **2.** When you have enough **material** for a story, you have enough ideas to write the story.

medusa   A **medusa** is an animal that lives in the sea: The **medusa** looks like it is made of jelly.

mussel   A **mussel** is an animal that lives in the sea. It has a black shell.

N

needle   A **needle** is a small, thin pin that is used for sewing: I like to watch the **needle** pull the thread in and out of the cloth.

pebble   A **pebble** is a very, very small stone: If you throw a **pebble** into the water, it will make a noise.

perform   When you do something while others watch, you **perform** for them: John can **perform** many songs. He plays well!

retrieve   To **retrieve** something is to bring it back: My dog never gets tired of **retrieving** sticks. He always brings the sticks back to me.

school of fish   A group of fish swimming together is called a **school of fish**: There were hundreds of little fish in that **school of fish**.

scissors   **Scissors** are a tool for cutting: Use the **scissors** to cut a piece of paper.

sea anemone   A **sea anemone** is a group of animals in the sea that sticks to rocks and other things: The **sea anemones** we saw looked like pretty plants.

shrunken   Something that has gotten smaller in size is **shrunken**: My sweater was so **shrunken** that I could not put it on.

splash	If you jump into a pool of water, the water will **splash**: I jumped into the pool. The water **splashed** everywhere.

spotlight	The **spotlight** is shining on the singer. The **spotlight** makes it easier to see her.

subway	A train that moves under the ground is called a **subway**: My older sister takes the **subway** to her school.

swallow	When you **swallow** food or a drink, it goes down your throat: She **swallowed** every last drop of milk in the glass.

tangle   To **tangle** things means to get them all twisted together and mixed up: Keep the pieces of string apart, so you don't **tangle** them.

tattered   Something that is ripped and has holes in it is **tattered**: We threw away the **tattered** shirt. It had too many holes in it.

taxi   A car that you pay to ride in is called a **taxi**: Sometimes when my mom is late for work, she takes a **taxi** instead of the bus.

tickle   Most people will laugh if you **tickle** them under the arm: The father **tickled** his son's foot.

train   When you **train** someone to do something, you teach them how to do it: My sister is **training** me to ride a bike.

triplets   Three children who are all born at the same time to the same parents are **triplets**: The **triplets** all have the same birthday.

wonderful   When you have a **wonderful** time, you have a very good time: We went to the movies to see our favorite cartoons. We had a **wonderful** time!

worn   After you use something or wear it for a long time, it becomes **worn**: He bought new pants because his old ones were so **worn**.

ACKNOWLEDGMENTS

For each of the selections listed below, grateful acknowledgment is made for permission to excerpt and/or reprint original or copyrighted material, as follows:

Selections

Enzo the Wonderfish, by Cathy Wilcox. Copyright © 1993 by Cathy Wilcox. Reprinted by permission of Ticknor & Fields Books for Young Readers, a division of Houghton Mifflin Company. All rights reserved.

"Family Treasure Chest," from May 1994 *Kid City* magazine. Copyright © 1994 by Children's Television Workshop. Reprinted by permission.

My Best Shoes, by Marilee Robin Burton, illustrated by James E. Ransome. Text copyright © 1994 by Marilee Robin Burton. Illustrations copyright © 1994 by James E. Ransome. Reprinted by permission of Tambourine Books, a division of William Morrow & Company, Inc.

One of Three, by Angela Johnson, illustrated by David Soman. Text copyright © 1991 by Angela Johnson. Illustrations copyright © 1991 by David Soman. Reprinted by permission of Orchard Books.

"Sea School," from June 1993 *Kid City* magazine. Copyright © 1993 by Children's Television Workshop. Reprinted by permission.

Selection from *Busy Buzzing Bumblebees,* by Alvin Schwartz. Copyright © 1982 by Alvin Schwartz. Reprinted by permission of HarperCollins Publishers.

Selection from *Daddies,* by Adele Aron Greenspun. Copyright © 1991 by Adele Aron Greenspun. Reprinted by permission of Philomel Books, a division of The Putnam & Grosset Book Group.

Selection from *Fish Faces,* by Norbert Wu. Copyright © 1993 by Norbert Wu. Reprinted by permission of Henry Holt and Company.

Selection from *Sharks,* by Erik D. Stoops and Sherrie Stoops, illustrated by Jeffrey L. Martin. Text copyright © 1994 by Erik D. Stoops and Sherrie Stoops. Reprinted by permission of Sterling Publishing Co., Inc., 387 Park Avenue South, New York, NY 10016. Illustrations copyright © 1994 by Jeffrey L. Martin. Reprinted by permission of the artist.

Selection from *That Family Circus Feeling,* by Bil Keane. Copyright © 1982 by Bil Keane. Reprinted by permission of King Features Syndicate.

Selection from *We're Home with the Family Circus,* by Bil Keane. Copyright © 1982, 1983, 1987 by Bil Keane. Reprinted by permission of King Features Syndicate.

Something from Nothing, by Phoebe Gilman. Copyright © 1992 by Phoebe Gilman. Reprinted by permission of Scholastic Canada Ltd.

Swimmy, by Leo Lionni. Copyright © 1963 by Leo Lionni. Reprinted by permission of Random House, Inc.

"What's It Like to Have a Family Reunion?" from December 1992 *Sesame Street Magazine.* Copyright © 1992 by Children's Television Workshop. Reprinted by permission.

Poetry

"A la víbora de la mar," traditional.

"Abuelita," by Tomás Allende Iragorri, from *Arcoiris de poesía infantil.* Copyright © 1987 by Editorial Universitaria. Reprinted by permission.

"Wish," by Dorothy Brown Thompson. Copyright © 1944 by Dorothy Brown Thompson. Reprinted by permission of University of Missouri-Kansas City Library.

Special thanks to Rhona St. Clair and Linda Riley of the New Jersey State Aquarium, Camden, New Jersey.

Special thanks to the following teachers whose students' compositions appear in the Be a Writer features in this level: Ellie Robertson, Elizabeth Stewart School, Pinole, California; Ashley Remeta, Perry Elementary School, Perry, Georgia.

CREDITS

Illustration 5, 11–34 James E. Ransome; 6, 38 Keiko Kasza; 7, 39 Glo Coalson; 2 (bottom left), 6, 41–70 Phoebe Gilman; 72–73 Fabricio Vanden Broeck; 76 Scott Bricher; 1, 2 (bottom right), 7, 80–108 David Soman; 117 Bil Keane; 8, 124 Ivan Chermayeff; 9, 125 S. D. Schindler; 2 (top left), 8, 126–156 Cathy Wilcox; 158 Katharyn Mary Fletcher; 159 Darcia Labrosse; 160–161, 163 Jefferey L. Martin; 164–165 Cortlan Carrillo; 166–167 Darius Detwiler; 9, 169–197 Leo Lionni; 199 Claudia de Teresa; 208 Dave Joly

Assignment Photography 35, 77 (background), 109–111, 116, 118–121 (borders), 158 (background), 198, 207 Banta Digital Group; 78–79 Kindra Clineff; 122–125 Dave DesRoches; 36–41, 112–117 (backgrounds), 126, 157, 168 Tony Scarpetta; 71, 77 (insets), 122–123 (inset), 158, 198 Tracey Wheeler

Photography 2 Pechter Photo (tr) 6 Steve Farrell (bottom cover) 8 Mike Nolan/Innerspace (b) 10 Keith I. Dixon (tl); Courtesy of Marilee R. Burton (mr); Courtesy of Marilee R. Burton (br) 34 Courtesy of James E. Ransome 40 Courtesy of Phoebe Gilman (l,r) 42 Scholastic Canada (m) 74-75 E.L.ee White 76 Steve Farrell (cover) 78 Orchard Books (l) 79 Courtesy of David Soman (r) 110 Courtesy of Caitlin Brownrigg 118 John Kailukiak/Institute of American Indian Arts Museum 119 Schalkwijk/Art Resource 120 Boston Athenaeum 121 Norman Rockwell Museum 157 Peter Solness (mr) 160 ©James Watt/Innerspace (tm); ©Norbert Wu/Innerspace (ml) 161 ©Doug Perrine/Innerspace 162 ©Mike Nolan /Innerspace (t); ©James D. Watt/Innerspace (br) 163 ©Doug Perrine/Innerspace 164 Cortlan Carrillo 200-201 Kyle Keener/Thomas H. Kean New Jersey State Aquarium 201 ©Steve Walker/Thomas H. Kean New Jersey State Aquarium (tr); ©Mike Price/Thomas H. Kean New Jersey State Aquarium (mr); ©Chris Lopez/Thomas H. Kean New Jersey State Aquarium (br) 202-7 © Norbert Wu 208 ©Alese & Morton Pechter/Pechter Photo (mr) 209 ©Alese & Morton Pechter/Pechter Photo (tm) 210-11 ©Alese & Morton Pechter/Pechter Photo (tm) 220 Chip and Maria Peterson (t); Flip Nicklin/Minden Pictures (m); © Bachmann/N.E. Stock Photo (b); 221 Lawrence Manning/Westlight 225 Chip and Maria Peterson (t) 227 PhotoEdit 228 John Alderson/Tony Stone Images, Chicago, Inc 229 © Robert K. Grubbs/N.E. Stock Photo

Here's what visitors to our Web site said about stories in *Discover.*

Something from Nothing was good because Joseph's grandfather was nice. He helped Joseph by making things out of his blanket. I am happy that Joseph's mother didn't throw away his things. I think other children would like to read this story. It made me feel good.

Treven Wong, Hawaii

Swimmy was a really good book. Swimmy helped all his friends swim out. It was exciting! I think a lot of people help others just like Swimmy did.

Erin Wrightson, Kentucky

Post your reviews in the

Kids' Clubhouse

at

www.eduplace.com